Tricking the *Eye*

by Stephanie Wilder

Editorial Offices: Glenview, Illinois • Parsippany, New Jersey • New York, New York
Sales Offices: Needham, Massachusetts • Duluth, Georgia • Glenview, Illinois
Coppell, Texas • Ontario, California • Mesa, Arizona

ISBN: 0-328-13459-7

5 6 7 8 9 10 V0G1 14 13 12 11 10 09 08 07

CONTENTS

Chapter 1 *Illusions and Animation*

What do you see in this picture?

Look again. Are your eyes playing a trick on you? How can one picture really be two pictures at the same time?

You are looking at an **optical illusion.** Optical illusions like this one make you wonder if your eyes are really seeing the things you think you see. Is that a picture of an old woman, or is it a young woman with her face turned away? As strange as it may seem, it is both!

Magicians use these types of tricks in their acts, but playing tricks on the eye is not just for magic shows. We may not realize it, but illusions are a big part of the cartoons we can see every day.

Cartoons are animated stories. We can see them everywhere. Some are drawn by hand, some are made using puppets and clay, and others are made using computers. But no matter how they are made, they are all based on the same idea. They all trick the eye.

In most animation, a group of still images, called **frames,** is put together to create the **illusion** of movement. Each still picture is just a little bit different from the one before. When they are seen rapidly one after another, it looks like the characters are actually moving. But it takes a lot of these still pictures to make a whole movie. It takes twenty-four different frames to make up only one second of a movie!

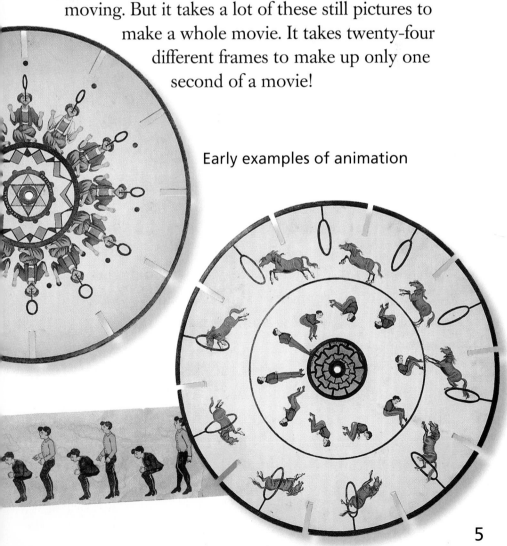

Early examples of animation

5

In the early days of cartoons, the many still pictures that make a cartoon had to be drawn by hand, and this took a lot of work. So animators came up with a few tricks to make their jobs easier.

Instead of drawing a whole new picture for every frame, they decided to draw only the parts of the picture that needed to move. Usually this meant making one background drawing. The characters were drawn on clear plastic sheets and laid over the

Cartoon animation uses two-dimensional drawings.

still background. The characters would change and look like they were moving, but only one background drawing was made. This method is called cel animation.

Another old trick is called the slash-and-tear system. Here the moving characters are drawn on regular paper, but then they are cut out. This way the different images of the moving characters can be placed on top of the background drawing. Either way, what you think you see is the characters coming to life.

There are many other ways to **animate.** One very simple way is stop-motion animation. With this method, clay models or puppets are photographed. Then they are moved just a little bit and photographed again. They are photographed at each stage of their action. The stills are then placed together in sequence, and it appears to the person watching that the models or puppets are moving on their own.

This trick is also used in movies with live actors. Before computers, special effects were done through simple camera tricks. If directors wanted to make something disappear, they would first film the scene with the object in it. Then they would stop the camera and remove the object. When the film started rolling again, it would appear as if the object had just vanished, like magic.

Stop-motion animation uses three-dimensional models instead of drawings.

So why do these simple tricks work? They are optical illusions. Your eyes are looking at an object, but your brain interprets it as something completely different.

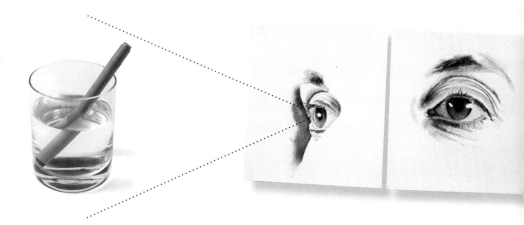

Actually, your eyes do not see at all. They just detect light and reflect it to your brain. Your brain does the seeing for you. Your brain takes the information that your eyes send, and it turns that information into something you can understand. Your brain can play some pretty funny tricks on you!

Your eye has three layers. The first layer is the sclera. This layer is the outside part of your eye. It is a protective layer. The middle layer is the choroid. This layer contains the muscles that help you focus. The last layer is the retina. Your retina contains cells called rods and cones. These are light-sensitive. Your retina is also the part of your eye that gives information to your brain.

The part of your eye that has color is called the iris. The pupil is the opening in the center of the iris. The iris adjusts the size of the pupil to let in the right amount of light. When it is dark, your iris shrinks, causing the pupil to expand. This lets in as much light as possible. When it is bright, your iris expands, making the pupil shrink. This prevents too much light from coming into your eye. The iris is just behind the cornea. The cornea is a clear layer over the iris and pupil.

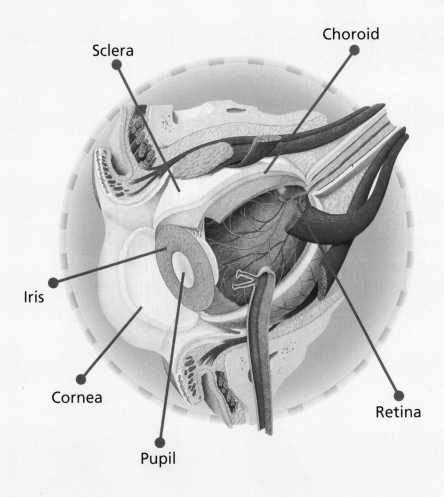

Choroid

Sclera

Iris

Cornea

Retina

Pupil

Animators use the camera to make you see just what they want you to see. The camera makes it seem as though still images are moving ones. Your eye, in some ways, works just like a camera. It essentially takes a picture of what is in front of you and gives it to your brain. Your brain's job is to figure out what image your eye has just given it.

Your eye turns light into images. Then it sends the information as nerve signals to your brain. It then displays them on your retina. Things that are far away are easy for your eyes to focus on, while things that are close to your eyes are harder to see. **Accommodation** is the word that scientists use for the act of focusing. Accommodation is when the lens gets flatter or rounder to bring the picture into focus on your retina.

When you were born, you could focus on things that were only 2½ inches from your face. But by the time you are about thirty years old, you will have to hold this book about six inches from your face in order to read it.

The picture that appears on your retina is actually upside down. It is your brain that takes that picture and turns it right side up. All this happens without you ever knowing about it.

Have you ever looked at the reflection of your face in the top of a spoon? It is upside down. The spoon reflects light in the same way that your eye does. This is because the shape of the spoon is **concave,** or bent inward, just like the shape of your eye. A concave lens curves inward. It disperses light rays. This means that when light rays strike a concave lens, the light spreads out and goes in many directions. Your eye's concave lens is what inverts images, or turns them upside down.

Just as the concave shape of the spoon on the left inverts the image, so does the eye's concave lens. (The spoon on the right shows the back.)

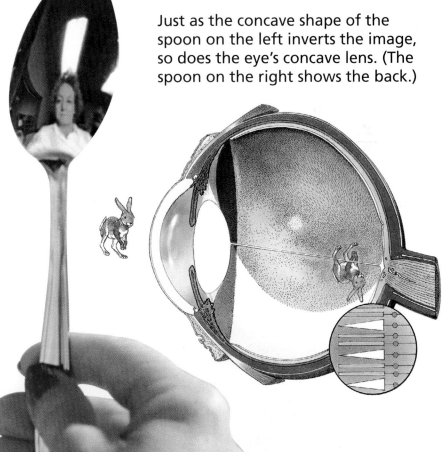

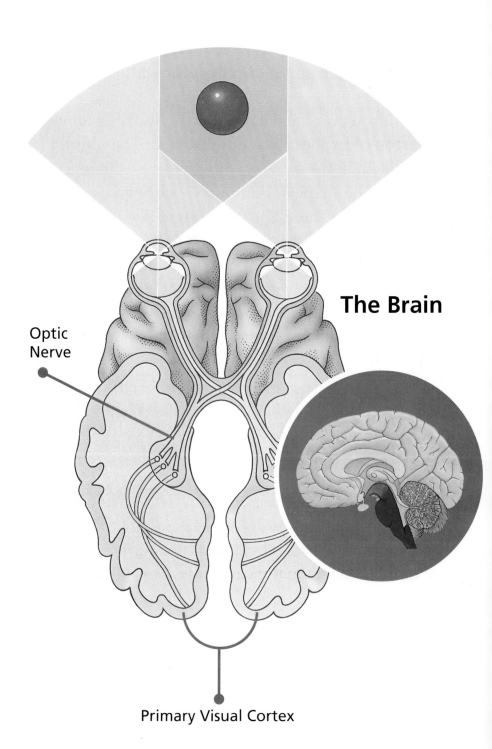

The Brain

Optic
Nerve

Primary Visual Cortex

When you see anything, the image you are seeing is light being reflected off the object. Light bounces off objects and travels though your eye. An upside-down image appears on your retina. Then the image is turned into an electrical signal that travels to your cerebral cortex.

The **cerebral cortex** is the part of your brain that receives signals from all your senses. The cerebral cortex has many parts, and interpreting electrical signals sent from the eye is just one of many jobs that this part of the brain does. The cerebral cortex recieves the signals that the eye sends to it and interprets them. When the signals arrive in the cerebral cortex, they are interpreted right side up. Your brain has turned the signal into an image that you can understand.

The ability of your brain to turn electrical signals into images that you can understand is what allows you to see things such as cartoons and magicians. But the tricks of the animators and magicians make the things you see seem real.

Chapter 3 *Computer Animation*

Cartoons from long ago used the tricks you read about earlier to make it seem as if still drawings were moving. Some cartoon creators of today still use these tricks, but many of them use the computer to help them create the illusion of movement.

Computer-assisted animation was the first form of computer animation. Artists use the computer to create still images and to make them come to life. This is two-dimensional computer animation. The computer is used to make a group of still images that begin to move only when they are put together. This uses the same principle that hand-drawn cartoons use. In this case the images are created on a computer screen instead of on a piece of paper. Each time the artists create an image, they make sure the new image looks slightly different from the image that came before it. This is how they make it seem like the character is moving.

A woman works in digital animation at Studio Ghibli in Tokyo. Studio Ghibli has produced such films as the Academy Award–winning *Spirited Away*.

Computer-generated animation of
the Mars rover from NASA

Another kind of computer animation is
computer-generated animation. Here the computer
creates an entire motion picture rather than a series of
still pictures.

Computer-generated animation can produce the
illusion of a three-dimensional world. Animators make
digital models of their characters and backgrounds.
They then give the computer the information needed
to make these models move on screen.

This type of animation is much more difficult for
the computer, but it is very real for the viewer. It makes
the world that the computer images have created seem
to come alive.

When you see a character made by the computer in three dimensions, it seems to move smoothly. It looks real and substantial on screen, as though it were a solid, living, breathing creature. It also gives the appearance that it is part of its background and not separated from it. A computer-assisted character sometimes looks less substantial and less real than a computer-generated character. It does not necessarily look like a living creature. It is not part of the background, since it is only in two dimensions. It seems to float in front of its surroundings.

The eye and the brain often do not perceive computer-assisted images as real. But computer-generated characters are more easily perceived as real. The illusion is complete when the artist convinces the viewer of this reality.

This animation was based on data taken from the rover's onboard sensors.

Chapter 4 *Optical Illusions*

Take a look at some of these optical illusions. Do any of these images seem to move? Is your **perception** of each of these pictures the truth? In the first optical illusion, do you see gray dots that appear and disappear where the white lines intersect? Are they really there? (They are not.) In the second optical illusion, do the black lines look wavy or straight? (They are perfectly straight.) In the third optical illusion, which of the center dots do you think is bigger? (They are the same size.) It is funny how your eyes can play tricks on your brain, isn't it?

Optical illusions, like the ones here and the one earlier in this book, can trick your brain into seeing something very different from what is actually drawn on the page. This type of illusion is the basic idea behind all of the cartoons we watch. Putting still images together and simply changing one or two details can make them appear to move. Computers can create the illusion of a substantial or living object. Other types of optical illusions can play the same tricks.

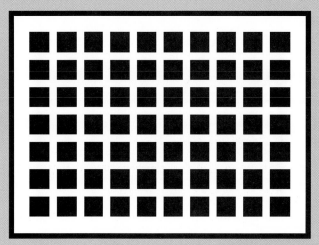
Hermann Grid

Optical Curve Illusion

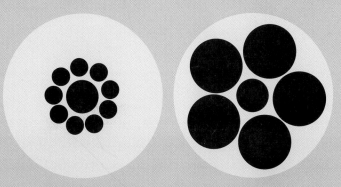
Van Ebbinghaus-Titchner Illusion

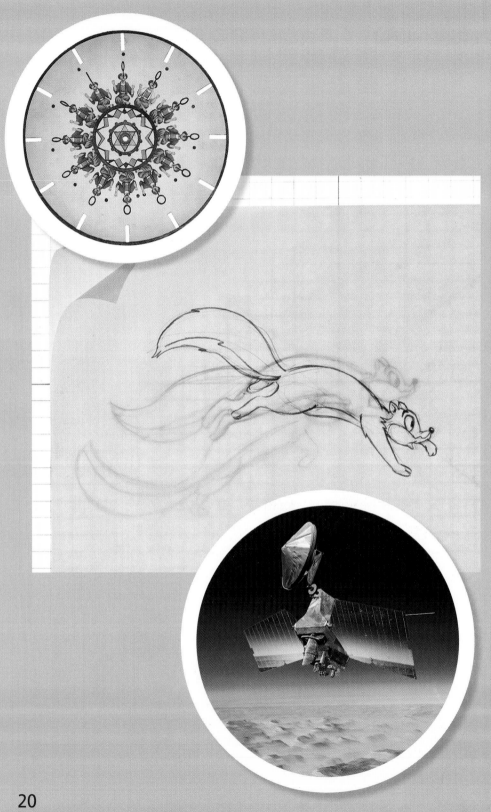

Conclusion

The creation of cartoons has come a long way. So has our understanding of our own brain.

Long ago, it was discovered that a group of still images put together could appear to move before your eyes. Animators started making this happen by drawing images on pieces of paper. Today, computers allow us to take this simple idea and create characters that seem to come to life on-screen. When we see this, we know that the characters we are seeing are not real. But the animators have many tricks that make the image seem real.

We now know that the eye can be fooled and that what you think you see might not be what is actually in front of you. Optical illusions are everywhere. Understanding how your eyes work and how the brain perceives images can help you to tell illusion from reality.

Now Try This

Make a Flip Book

As we have already learned, the first cartoons were made by putting a series of still images together to make them look as if they were moving. Now it is your turn to make your own cartoon. The flip book was one of the first kinds of cartoon. Making a flip book is easy and fun.

Here's How to Do It!

1. First, you need to gather your materials. The easiest way to get started is to find a small, empty notebook. (If you don't have one, don't worry. Take several pieces of blank paper and cut them into equal-sized pieces. Next, staple them together on the left-hand side to make a book.) You will also need markers, crayons, or pencils to draw your cartoon.

2. Begin by drawing a picture on the first page of your notebook. This can be a picture of anything that you would like to see moving, such as an animal, person, robot, or boat.

3. Next, draw the same picture on the second page. This time make a very small change in the direction of the movement you want to create.

4. Continue drawing the picture, changing it just a little bit each time, until the movement is complete. The more pictures you draw, the longer your cartoon will be.

5. Finally, after you have finished each drawing, hold the book with your left hand and flip through it very fast with your right hand. Watch as your drawings come to life!

Glossary

accommodation *n.* the automatic adjustment of the lens of the eye to see objects at various distances.

animate *v.* to make lively.

cerebral cortex *n.* part of the brain that receives signals from the senses.

computer-assisted animation *n.* two-dimensional computer animation; a series of still computer images put together to create movement.

computer-generated animation *n.* the process by which a computer uses models and formulas to make a still image move in lifelike ways, often in three dimensions.

concave *adj.* curved inward.

frames *n.* individual still images that make up a cartoon.

illusion *n.* something that appears to be different from what it actually is.

optical illusion *n.* illusion having to do with sight or seeing.

perception *n.* the brain's understanding of something.